Handwriting

Here's a short note to parents:
It is recommended that an adult spends time
with a child while doing any kind of school practice,
to offer encouragement and guidance. Find a quiet place
to work, preferably at a table, and encourage your child to hold
his or her pen or pencil correctly. Try to work at your child's
pace and avoid spending too long on any one page or
activity. Most of all, emphasise the fun element of
what you are doing and enjoy this special
and exciting time!

Designed and illustrated by Jeannette O'Toole
Cover design by Dan Green
Educational consultant Nina Filipek

Autumn
Publishing

Shapes

Find the stickers and put them in place.

Start at the dot and trace over the dashes to draw these shapes.

Try to keep your pencil on the paper for the whole time.

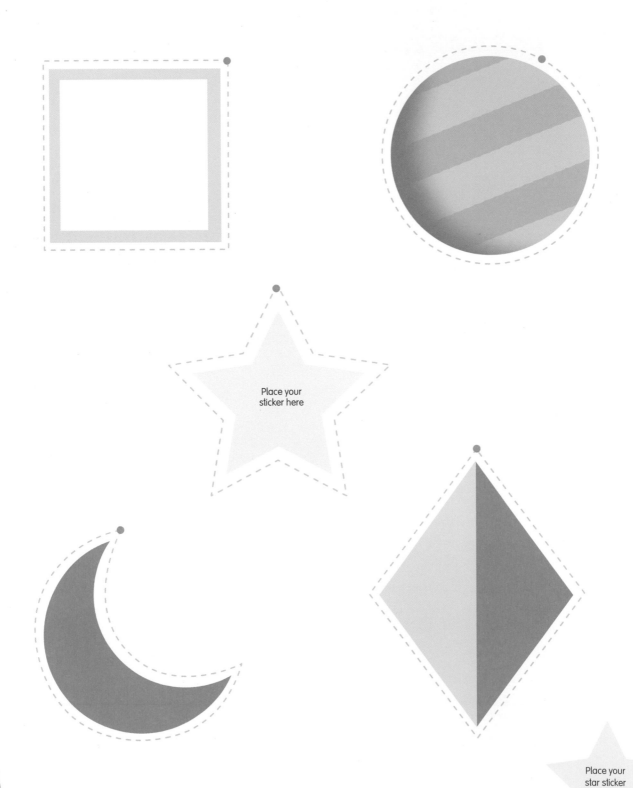

Place your sticker here

Place your star sticker here

Place your
sticker here

Place your
star sticker
here

Writing patterns

Find the stickers and put them in place. Start at the dots and trace over the dashes to the creature at the end of each line.

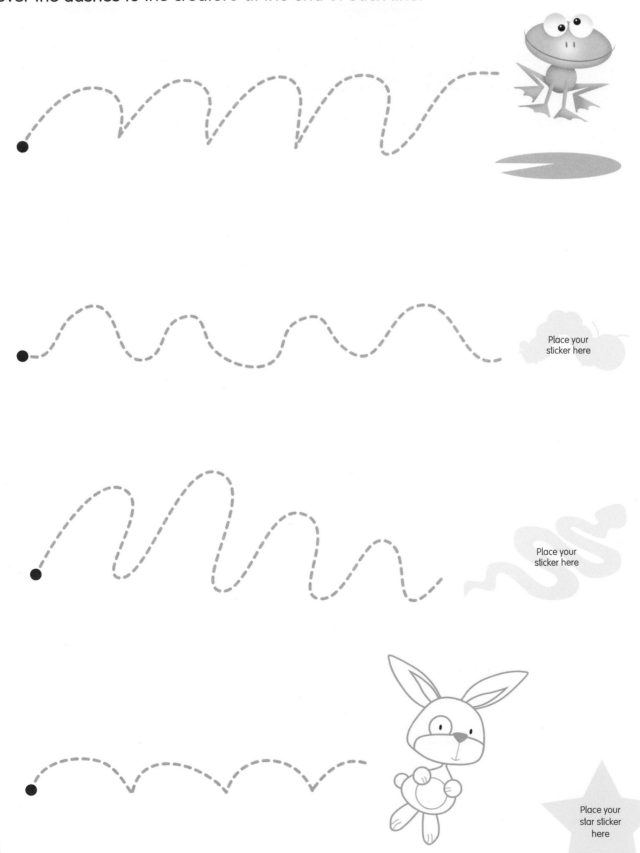

Place your
sticker here

Place your
sticker here

Place your
star sticker
here

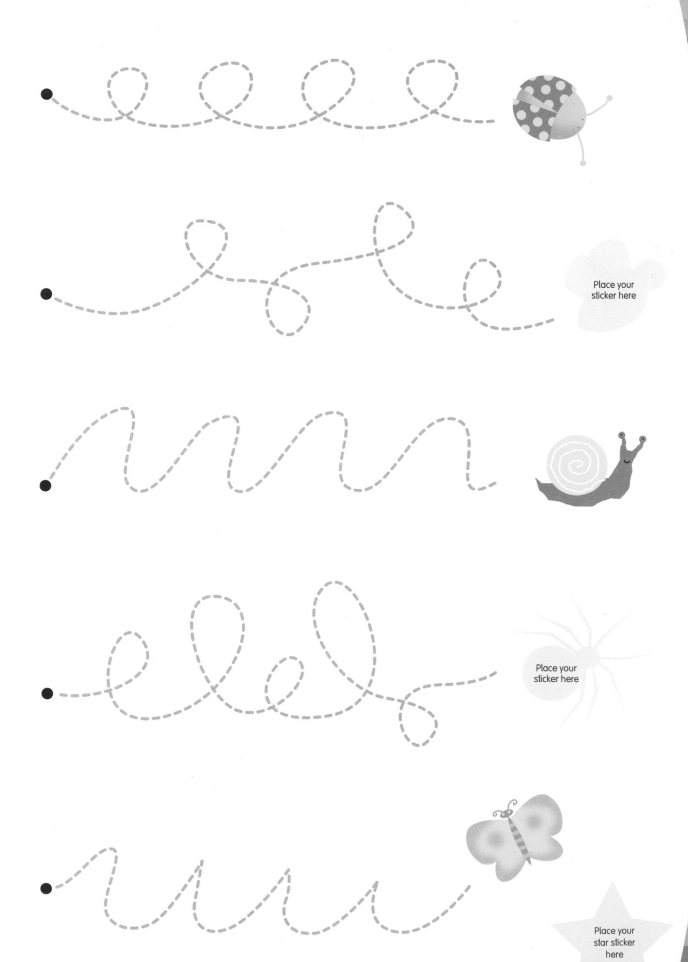

Place your
sticker here

Place your
sticker here

Place your
star sticker
here

Writing patterns

Start at the dot. Look at the direction of the arrows and trace over the dashes. Then write the patterns yourself.

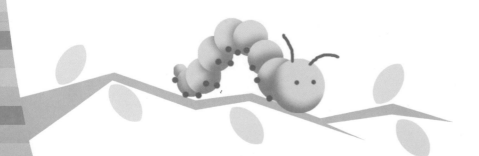

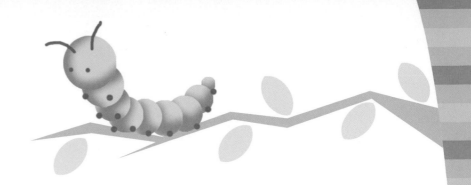

MMM /MMMMMMMM

UUU uuuuuuuuu

CCoo CCoo CCoo

Letter patterns – straight lines and curves

Look at the direction of the arrows and trace over the dashes.
Then write the letters yourself.

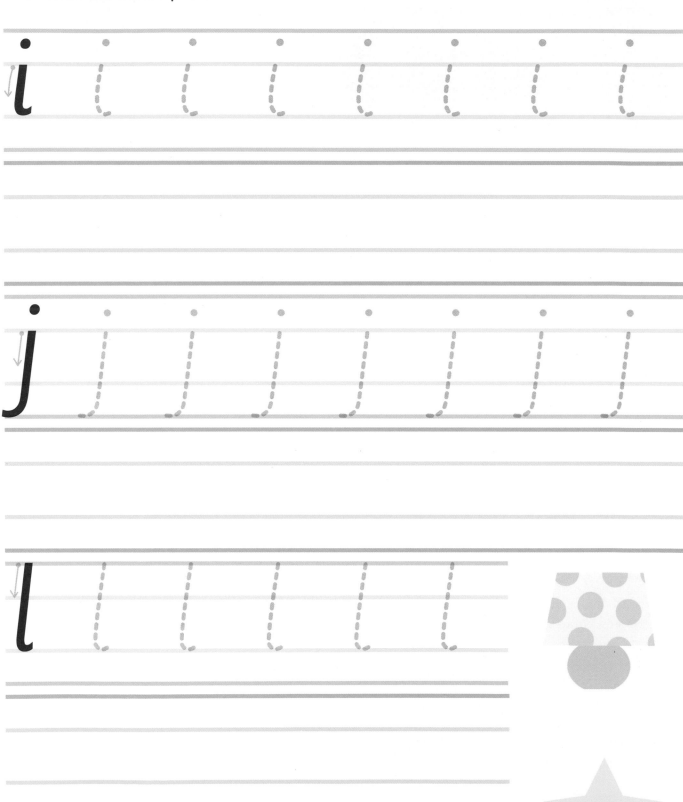

i i i i i i i i

j j j j j j j j

l l l l l l

t t t t t t t t

u u u u u u u u

y y y y y y y

Letter patterns –
up and down strokes

Look at the direction of the arrows and trace over the dashes.
Then write the letters yourself.

n n n n n n n n n

m m m m m m m m

r r r r r r r r

h h h h h h h h h

b b b b b b b b

p p p p p p p

Letter patterns – half circle and circle

Look at the direction of the arrows and trace over the dashes.
Then write the letters yourself.

a a a a a a a a a

d d d d d d d d

g g g g g g

c c c c c c c c c

q q q q q q q q q

e e e e e e e e

o o o o o o o o

Place your star sticker here

Complex letters

Look at the direction of the arrows and trace over the dashes.
Then write the letters yourself.

s s s s s s s s

f f f f f f f f

w w w w w w

k k k k k k k k k k k k k k

v v v v v v v v v v v v v v

x x x x x x x x x x x x

z z z z z z z z z z z

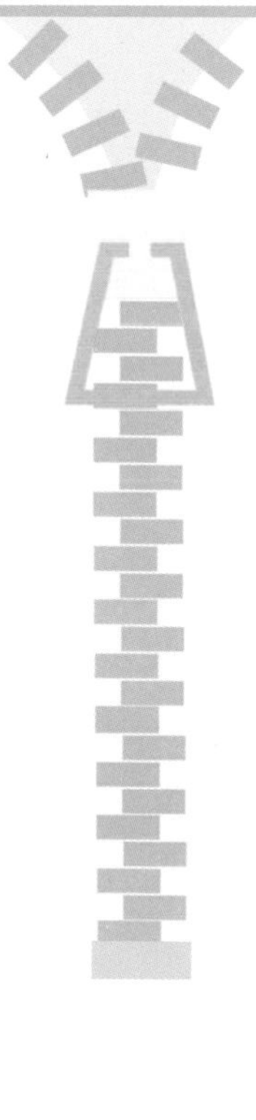

Place your star sticker here

Letter formation

Find the missing letter stickers and put them in place.
Trace and copy the letters of the alphabet.

a b c

Place your sticker here

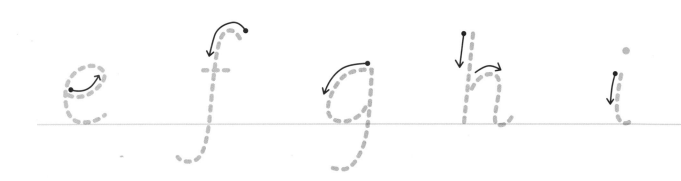

e f g h i

j

Place your sticker here

l m

Place your star sticker here

n   o

Place your
sticker here

q

r   s   t   u   v

w

Place your
sticker here

y   z

Place your
star sticker
here

Joining strokes

To do joined-up writing you add **exit** strokes at the base of some letters.
Trace over the dashes, then write the letters yourself.

i l k u m

i l k u m

n a d e t c

n a d e t c

Place your
star sticker
here

Joining strokes

Letters based on a half-circle or circle can have joining strokes at the **beginning**.
Trace over the dashes, then write the letters yourself.

a   c   d   g   o   q

a   c   d   g   o   q

Practise:

ad   do   oc   ag

ad   do   oc   ag

Place your
star sticker
here

Joining strokes

Some letters have exit strokes at the **top** of the letter.
Trace over the dashes, then write the letters yourself.

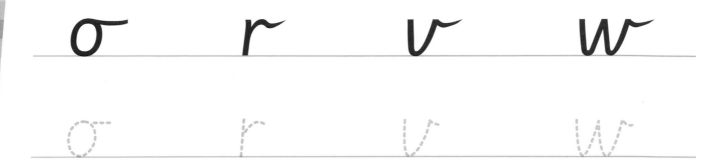

o   r   v   w

Practise:

oo   rrr   vv   ww

Place your
star sticker
here

Joining strokes

The letters **f** and **t** sometimes have different kinds of joining strokes.
Trace over the dashes, then write the letters yourself.

f or *f*   *f*   *f*

t or *t*   *t*   *t*

Practise:

fl   *ef*   *tu*   *tr*

fl   *ef*   *tu*   *tr*

Some letters can be joined with a loop, or they can be left unjoined.

g or *g*   *j* or *j*   *y* or *y*

g *g*   *j* *j*   *y* *y*

Place your
star sticker
here

Joining strokes

This is how to join the remaining letters of the alphabet. These letters can be joined or left unjoined. Trace over the dashes, then write the letters yourself.

p   b   z   x   s

ph   br   bl

ph   br   bl

ox   box   zoo

ox   box   zoo

Place your star sticker here

Pairs of joined-up letters

Find the stickers and put them in place. Here are some examples of pairs of joined-up letters. Trace over the dashes, then write the words on the lines.

poppy

kitten

lorry

moon

teddy

geese

Practise joined-up writing

Find the stickers and put them in place. Copy the words on the lines under each picture. Try to keep your pencil on the paper for the whole time.

a puppy and a poppy

a [Place your sticker here] *and a mitten*

Place your star sticker here

a [Place your sticker here] and a balloon

a frog sits on a log

Place your star sticker here

Capital letters

Copy the letters of the alphabet as capital letters.
Find the missing letter stickers.

A B **Place your sticker here** D

E F G H I

J **Place your sticker here** L M

Place your
star sticker
here

N  O P

Place your
sticker here

 R Place your
sticker here T  U V

W  X Y Z

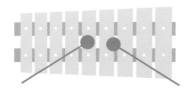  

Place your
star sticker
here

Practise capital letters

Write the capital letters for the days of the week and the months on the opposite page. Then find the missing letter stickers.

_unday

Place your sticker here onday

_uesday

_ednesday

_hursday

Place your sticker here riday

_aturday

Place your star sticker here

_pril

uly

ctober

_ecember

Find the stickers and put them in place. Copy the sentences under each picture. Write them on the lines.

Place your sticker here skip in April.

_____

_____

Place your sticker here

Painting is on Monday.

_____

_____

Place your star sticker here

Place your
sticker here

We play football on Wednesdays.

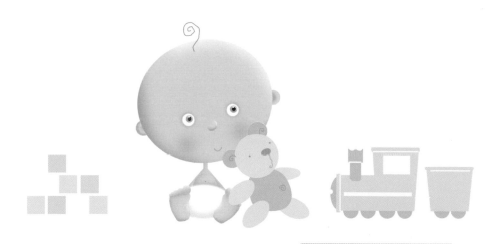

The baby likes Place your sticker here .

Place your
star sticker
here

Writing sentences

Find the stickers and put them in place. Write the sentences on the lines.

The [Place your sticker here] dog loves to run.

_____

_____

Parties are great fun!

_____

_____

Place your
star sticker
here

Hello Kitty is...
Sleeping Beauty

HarperCollins *Children's Books*

Hello Kitty is...

Sleeping Beauty

Dear Daniel is...

the handsome prince

Tippy is...

the king

Mimmy is...

the queen

Cast

Thomas is...
a good fairy

Tracy is...
a good fairy

Timmy and Tammy are...
good fairies

Fifi is...
the naughty fairy

Hello Kitty and her friends
are performing in a new play.

They're about to put on their
costumes and take to the stage.

Ladies and gentlemen,
girls and boys, it's time for...
Sleeping Beauty!

Once upon a time, in the kingdom of Foreverland, there lived a king and queen.

They were very happy, and grew
even happier when they had a
baby girl, a beautiful princess.

Ta Daaaaa!

The king and queen were overjoyed to have a child. They threw a grand party to celebrate.

There were four good fairies in the land and the king and queen invited them all to the party. Unfortunately they forgot to invite a naughty fairy, who also lived in the kingdom.

The good fairies gifted the princess with special wishes.

Ting!
Wisdom!

Ting!
Beauty!

Ting!
Kindness!

Ting!
Great baking skills!

The naughty fairy was
very upset that she was not
invited to the party, and she
did not wish the princess well.

Instead, she wished that when the princess turned sixteen she would
prick her finger on a spinning wheel and fall asleep for a hundred years.

The king and queen were very worried
about the naughty fairy's bad wish.

They loved the princess so much that they kept her protected at all times.

The princess grew to be kind, wise and beautiful,
and she baked amazing cakes.

One day, just after her sixteenth birthday, she slipped out of the palace for a walk in the grounds.

At the edge of the palace grounds,
the princess came across a spinning
wheel. She had never seen one before,
and reached out to touch it.

As soon as she touched the wheel,
she pricked her finger, and suddenly
fell into a deep sleep.

The good fairies saw what had happened, and carried the princess to her bed. They did not want her to be alone, so they decided to put the whole kingdom under a spell, to also sleep for a hundred years.

The king and queen fell asleep, as did all of their subjects. All of the animals and birds slept too.

As the years passed, a large forest
grew up around the kingdom.

Eventually, a handsome prince arrived from a far away land. He asked what was beyond the forest and was told that a beautiful princess, known as Sleeping Beauty, slept in the palace.

He vowed to reach her.

The prince struggled through the forest and made his way into the castle. He discovered the princess asleep in her chamber and thought she was the most beautiful girl he had ever seen. He kissed her.

At that exact moment, the princess woke from her slumbers.
The hundred years had passed.
"Are you my prince?" she asked. "I've been dreaming about you."

The king and queen woke too, as did all of their subjects and the animals and birds. The whole kingdom was awake!

As time passed, Sleeping Beauty and the prince fell deeply in love.
The prince proposed and Sleeping Beauty accepted.
The two were wed in the castle gardens.

And, of course, they lived
happily ever after.

The End

Hooray!

Hooray!

The audience applauds loudly.
The play is a super success.

Hooray!

Hooray!

After all that acting Hello Kitty feels very tired. 'I might have a snooze later,' she thinks,

'although maybe not for a hundred years...'

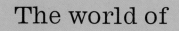

The world of Hello Kitty

Enjoy all of these wonderful Hello Kitty books.

Picture books

Occasion books

Where's Hello Kitty?

Activity books

...and more!

Hello Kitty and friends story book series